BOOKS TO BUCKS

The Top 20 Ways to Make Money from Your Book

(even if you haven't written it yet)

2nd Edition

by Everett O'Keefe & Jenn Foster

The Top 20 Ways to Make Money from Your Book, (even if you haven't written it yet).

SECOND EDITION

©2015, 2023 Everett O'Keefe & Jenn Foster

ALL RIGHTS RESERVED. This book contains material protected under International and Federal Copyright Laws and Treaties. Any unauthorized reprint or use of this material is prohibited. No part of this book may be reproduced or transmitted in any form or by any means electronic or mechanical including photocopying, recording, or by any information storage and retrieval system without express written permission from the author/publisher.

In association with:
Elite Online Publishing
63 East 11400 South
Suite #230
Draper, UT 84020
EliteOnlinePublishing.com

Ignite Press
5070 N 6th, Suite 189
Fresno CA 93710
IgnitePress.us

ISBN: 978-1-956642-96-4

QUANTITY PURCHASES: Schools, companies, professional groups, clubs, and other organizations may qualify for special terms when ordering quantities of this title. Copies of this publication may be ordered from: email info@eliteonlinepublishing.com

All rights reserved by EVERETT O'KEEFE & JENN FOSTER
This book is printed in the United States of America.

Books to Bucks

Register This Book and Get Free Updates and a Money Mind Map

Things change rapidly in the publishing world! If you register your copy of this book, we will keep you up to date about the ever-changing ways to leverage your book. PLUS, we will send you our custom infographic, your "mind map" for making money with a book!

Visit AuthorJennFoster.com/books-to-bucks

TABLE OF CONTENTS

INTRODUCTION	1
1 - CAPTURING LEADS	11
2 - THE 100 PAGE FLYER	17
3 - USE YOUR BOOK AS A BUSINESS CARD	21
4 - THE PERFECT GIFT	25
5 - GETTING PAST THE GATEKEEPER	29
6 - GET SPEAKING GIGS	33
7 - BACK OF ROOM SALES	39
8 - YOUR BOOK AS OFFICE DÉCOR	43
9 - LET PEOPLE KNOW ABOUT YOUR BOOK	47
10 - ELEVATOR SPEECH	51
11 - PRESS RELEASE	55
12 - SELLING AT ONLINE BOOKSTORES	59
13 - SELLING ON YOUR WEBSITE	63

14 - USING YOUR BOOK AT A TRADE SHOW	**67**
15 - YOUR BOOK AS AN ESCALATION STRATEGY	**71**
16 - FREE GIVEAWAY	**75**
17 - EVENT CONTEST WHEN SPEAKING OR PRESENTING	**79**
18 - NEW AND BETTER OPPORTUNITIES	**85**
19 - MEDIA ATTENTION	**91**
20 - JOINT VENTURES	**99**
BONUS CHAPTERS	**103**
21 - INCREASE YOUR FEES	**105**
22 - CLOSE MORE DEALS	**109**
23 - PRE-LAUNCHING BOOKS	**113**
CONCLUSION	**117**
ABOUT THE AUTHORS	**121**

INTRODUCTION

There are surveys that indicate that 81% of people have a book in them and want to get it out to the world. If you think about those numbers, that's over 200 million people in the United States. The truth of the matter is that most people will never finish a book, and those people who do finish a book will never actually leverage that book properly. One of the things we want to do with this book is put together several different solutions that people can utilize to monetize the book that they either already created or that they are in the process of creating.

Out of those millions of people, many have written books that are on their computer or printed out from a typewriter sitting somewhere in their house and have never been published. Now is the time to take advantage of the self-publishing platform online and get their book published.

There are also several books that people have on yellow legal pads or in notebooks that are cluttering their bookshelves. There are journals that people have kept that they'd love to turn into books; there are so many different things out there that people would love to get out to the world, or to just get out to their families. The beautiful thing with kindle Direct Publishing, Ingram and other online self-publishing platforms and print-on-demand is that now they have a way to do that.

A friend of mine who's also a business coach, Timmy, his mother has for years scribbled down cute little poems on pieces of paper, and she's been collecting these for decades. Last year, he gathered them all together, typed them up, went into Kindle Direct Publishing and created a book unbeknownst to his mom. On her birthday, he had copies of the book printed, elected to have them distributed and then presented a copy to her as well as to all the siblings in the family.

Through the power of current publishing tools, she was incredibly touched, and the family has an instant and completely professional memoir. Now his mother is a published author and is tickled pink about it.

That is one great example of the power of these new publishing methods and how accessible they are to all of us.

Timmy typed up all his mother's poems, but with the technology we have today and all of the resources that are available to us, if you have a journal or any kind of handwritten document, you can scan that into your computer as a PDF and have someone transcribe it for you at minimal costs or even transcribe it yourself. With the technology out there to do all of this, it is just so simple that it's ridiculous. Not long ago it would have taken forever to type up someone's book, not so with all the dragon software and the different software options to translate or transcribe that are available today. There are so many ways that we can leverage the technology today to make it simple for us to get our books published.

So really, the days of having to sit down with your pencil and paper or your old IBM typewriter or even your modern word processing, the days of having to sit down and write or type a book are largely behind us.

We aren't trying to say that there isn't a time and a place for someone who wants to create a book in the old fashion way. We recognize the artistry that goes into a well-crafted novel, the creativity that goes into a tight and precise poem and that those things are not going to be easily replaced simply by dictation or voice-activated software.

We realize this completely. But for most people, the book that is sitting inside of them is much more likely to come out and see the light of day if people can simply leverage technologies like voice-activated software by recording their audio and then later having it transcribed. Or by recording themselves on video and then having the video content transliterated into a book. It's these methods that are going to allow people, who would never spend the countless hours necessary on a Word processor, to get their message out to the world.

We are completely excited about this age of publishing that is in front of us. We are going to watch people who had these messages buried inside them that they've been dying to get out to the world make it happen. We are going to see these explode upon the world stage, and it really is ushering in a whole new age of publishing.

Ultimately, what's going on now in publishing is as transformational as the creation of the Gutenberg press. In the same way that that press allowed books to be mass produced instead of being written in longhand by scribes in dark little cells; instead of books being incredibly expensive to buy and taking so long to create, with the Gutenberg press, they could be mass produced. This is the new Gutenberg press. Amazon, print-on-demand publishing, (Kindle Direct Publishing) or IngramSpark are the Gutenberg press of the 21st Century, and it's so exciting to watch this happen.

Here's the deal. It turns out that U.S. consumers are spending nearly an hour a day reading books online, that's an incredible statistic (2013 Media Use Benchmark Study). According to Forbes this is really reflected in what's going on at Amazon where they are earning $5.25 billion a year in annual revenue. Now the trick is that the number is going to continue to increase.

For example, right now, approximately 30% of all Americans have some sort of e-reading device, but that number is steadily growing every day as more and more people gravitate to their smart phones; they gravitate to their tablets and every other device that can read books online.

Think about the process of finding and purchasing a book. Prior to Amazon, we would first have to hear about a book, we might hear about it from talking to a friend or listening to the radio or watching a television show. We'd hear about a book, and then we'd think, "Gosh, I'd actually like to have that book." But we weren't going to be able to find and purchase that book that day because we were out running around, or we had other time constraints. So on the next day or sometime later in the week, we'd end up going to a bookstore to actually get that book.

Then of course, once we're at the bookstore, we've had to take some time to find that book, searching the racks, asking the cashier or someone else to help us find it, etc. And let's say they've got it, great; we buy it; we take it home. If they don't have it, then we have to have the clerk order that specific book. And in the old model, we might have to wait a week or two for that book to show up, if it's even available.

Now compare that to what the process is right now. Currently, the process is pretty much instantaneous. We hear about a book on the radio, a friend tells us about it, we see it on a TV show, or we read about it online. We literally can go to Amazon, use the Amazon One Click feature and have that book immediately downloaded to our tablet, to our phone, even to our laptop or desktop, if we want.

It's not like we must limit ourselves to having an actual Kindle device. Now with the free applications that Amazon provides for almost every single electronic plat- form, we can now read our Kindle book relatively instantly on anything. It really is rather incredible. Now this shortened sales cycle means people are buying and consuming a ton more books.

I know that we, as authors, are going through many, many more books than we ever did before. Our target audience is going through more and more books than before simply because of the ease of use and the cost. We used to have to pay anywhere between $15 and $25 for a physical copy of a book that we acquired at the bookstore. Now we can get that exact same content digitally for anywhere from $3 to $10 depending upon the book.

So not only have things become much faster, but they've also become much cheaper and much more convenient for us to consume, which really takes us to another point, now we can carry our library with us. We no longer have to decide which book to take on vacation, which book to have with us, so we can read at lunch, during work, at the doctor's appointment or any other place imaginable; we can actually carry our whole book library with us in our pocket.

When you add up all these different factors, you can see the reason that book consumption is growing substantially, and why we expect it to continue to grow. It's odd because this is a time where you would think with the prevalence of online video and all these other different, very engaging mediums or media; you think the opposite would be true, but that's not the case, and now you see why.

So with book readership raising because the convenience of reading is getting easier and easier every day, and the cost of buying books is getting lower and lower every day, you can see why it's important for you to not only have a book, but also to have a strategy in place to leverage that book for your financial benefit; that really is the crux of the reason behind this book. We have put this book together to give you numerous ways to make money with the book that you're either writing, you've written or that you have yet to write.

We're going to give you several strategies, some obvious and some less than obvious, so that you can leverage your book in as many ways as possible or in the ways that best suit your book and your goals. So read on to the following chapters and keep an open mind as we give you some unusual and effective means to making money with your book.

1 - CAPTURING LEADS

Among the many, many ways to make money with a book, perhaps the most important and the most fundamental thing for you to remember is that you need to plan. This ensures that your book is a lead-capturing magnet. There are many ways to do this, but we want to talk about some very basic and obvious ways, so that you will not skip this important step. We've intentionally made this the number one step because it affects all the other ways to make money with your book that we'll be discussing in later chapters.

So how do you capture leads with a book? Well, the most obvious way and a way that people have done for ages is to simply make sure you have your contact information in your book. You simply include your business address, a phone number, or an email in the bio section of your book. You could leverage the cover to imply your book brand or your website. You need to do some- thing, so that people can find you. The one thing that you don't want to happen is for someone to read your book, love your book and then have no way to find you.

Now, a more modern method of lead capture is to put a lead capture device in your book, so that people can text or email in to get information or bonuses and become part of an auto-responder funnel. If you're unfamiliar with an autoresponder, that is simply a pre- programmed set of emails that go out in response to somebody's action. That action may be that they text their name and information to a phone number or that they email you or they make a phone call. The autoresponder simply responds by sending one or more auto- mated emails on or after that point.

The importance of capturing leads is to build your list, and the importance of having your book is to build a list of followers or a list of people who like you and trust you and want to keep following you. To do that, you need to have a call-to-action in your book of a way for them to find you.

For example, in a well thought out book that has considerable lead capture, you might see something like this. The author might put in a call to action to get a bonus. Let's say it's a free chapter, or it's an audio interview, or access to an online webinar or live event. The author may say, "In order to get more information, go ahead and text your name and email address to 555-555-5555." It could also say to visit a particular website or call a particular number and leave your name and email.

When the person visits the website, for instance, they might encounter a video of the author talking about any bonuses and at that point be given an opportunity to opt in to receive these bonuses.

For example, visit Yourwebsite.com or text "keyword" to 55555 with your name and email, or text your name and email address to 555-555-5555, or email us at register@yourwebsite.com

Now adding a call to action in your book and a lead capture mechanism in your book is fundamental to everything you will do with your book. If you skip this and fail to execute on this, then you are missing a golden opportunity. We recognize that some people reading this book already have their book out "in the wild," and obviously, you're not able to make alterations to that book because it's already in people's hands. We understand this, and we know that you are kicking your- self now because you missed some opportunities to place calls to action or lead capture mechanisms in your book. Don't fret. Just make sure that your next book or next revision includes calls to action. In fact, make sure that the calls to action occur multiple times in your book.

I have seen authors include calls to action at the front of their book and at the back of their book and somewhere in between. We've also seen people include calls to action at the end of every chapter. You can determine what's appropriate for your audience and for the offerings that you may want to give to people. But what- ever you do, include effective, powerful calls to action. While we are on this topic, what are effective calls to action?

If you're writing a fiction book, and you have a very passionate readership; a bonus chapter or some unusual piece of back story may be very effective. Or including ideas and thoughts along the lines of the "making of" or "behind the scenes" about how you created a certain character or how you came up with a certain plot line. All of this may be very powerful in a fiction work.

In a non-fiction piece, it could be an additional strategy or an additional tool; it could be an audio interview of you. You could utilize some video training or a PDF or mind map that you've created and some incentive to get people to opt in to your list. You could also utilize a drawing or contest, but please make sure that you do so in accordance with any laws that may apply when running contests or promotions.

For the PDF, you could also do a workbook type PDF

where they have to go through certain steps and fill it out, like a free workbook, to go along with your how-to, if your book is a non-fiction how-to book.

We have even seen authors give away free copies of the audio book that the person is reading, so that the reader can consume it either by audio or in written text. Whatever you do, just come up with a compelling bonus, so that it really is an effective call to action.

Now keep this in mind, a number of the people who read your book may have been given this book. They may not know who you are; they may not know who your company is, and they may not know anything about you. As they're reading your book and learning more about you, this is when the light bulb will be going off in their head, and they will be thinking that they need to get in touch with you.

Therefore, you want to make it as easy as possible for them to do so. Make sure your calls to action appear multiple times in your book and then of course, your contact info is readily available as well.

2 - THE 100 PAGE FLYER

One very effective way to leverage your book is what we like to call *The 100-Page Flyer*. So many people, when they go into a business or meet with a potential customer, give them a trifled flyer or some other thin piece of paper as a leave behind. Well, one great advantage of a book is that it has what we like to call, "Thud Factor." Meaning that, if you drop this on someone's desk, it has a nice gratifying thud to it; it gets attention, and it's so much better than the typical flyer or other promotional piece that so many businesspeople use.

In today's economy, as an author, you should be able to get copies of your book for relatively little money. Ultimately, books nowadays tend to run anywhere from about $2.50 to about $6 a copy for most author copies. (By the way, if you are paying substantially more than this, then you might want to get in touch with us for some other fulfillment methods).

When you think about the cost of a book, it's relatively minimal. Think about how much time and ef- fort you expend getting an appointment with somebody. You spend a lot more money, whether it's hard money or not, setting up an appointment. You've had to develop the relationship to set that appointment; you've had to make phone calls; you may have had to travel, whether it's across town or across the country. You've expended a lot of effort to make that appointment happen.

Don't try to seal the deal with a flyer that you printed out for 50 cents on your computer or paid a dollar for at a printer. It doesn't make sense to shortchange yourself at that point. Instead, go the Cadillac route and give them your 100-page book. Give them your 100-page fly- er and allow your book to impress them. At $3 to $6 a copy, it makes no sense whatsoever to keep the books in your trunk or in your office. They need to be on your prospects and customers desks.

We like to think of books as arrows in your quiver. The arrows in your quiver are great tools; they are weapons for you to use; they are things at your disposal. But they do no good if they are still in your quiver at the end of the day. You need to pull the arrow out, put it in the bow and launch it. Your book cannot be effective unless you put it in people's hands, and this is one way to do so.

It really does leave such an impact to the person that you're giving it to. No one else is doing this; your competition isn't doing this. There are a few people who can say, "I'm a published author." If you are leaving your book, that's going to make such an impact, more impact than any type of flyer that they're going to toss in the garbage. Because your competition isn't doing this, you are going to have a large jump on them, and your credibility and trust levels will soar.

Another wonderful thing about books is that people don't throw them away. Flyers get thrown away; business cards get thrown away; books do not get thrown away. Even if someone doesn't necessarily intend to read a book, it will habitually stay on their desk for a very long time. And even when they ultimately think that they want to get it off the desk, they'll often put it on a bookshelf, and it will sit on the book shelf for a long time.

Everett has books sitting on his desk that he has had for years that he probably will never read. Many of these books have been given to him, but he just can't bring himself to throw them away. You see, books are priceless; books are worth far more than the paper that they are printed on, and it just seems criminal to throw them away. It's like wasting great ideas. Even if we don't necessarily agree with those ideas all the time, we just can't bring ourselves to throw them away.

So would you like to have that kind of sticking power on your prospect's and customer's desk? Would you like for them to repeatedly bump into your book when they are perusing their desk? Think of the reason that people give away free pens and calculators; it's to keep top-of- mind awareness; it's so that people will constantly or frequently be reminded of somebody.

Well, the great thing about a book is it does that at a higher level. It's not cheap or crass like a $1 pen or a $4 calculator. It seems like it's a gift of value that hangs around for a long, long time. Even though you know that it costs you $3, let's say, the recipient doesn't know that it only costs you that, and anyway, a book is always worth far more than the cost of the book.

As a case in point, Everett was given a book when he went to a local Chamber of Commerce event. The person who was speaking at the event gave him a copy of the book, and it was really to help promote her business and brand. Well, that event was three years ago, and that book is still sitting on Everett's bookshelf staring at him anytime he goes through his books, talk about sticking power!

3 - USE YOUR BOOK AS A BUSINESS CARD

Using a book instead of your business card, or alongside your business card, is perhaps one of the most powerful ways that you can use your book. When you are at a networking event, and someone asks you for a business card, don't just give them your business card. Go ahead and give them a copy of your book, and then watch their expression. They will be simply surprised and, in some cases, blown away. You see, nobody does this.

First, very few people are authors and even have that opportunity to give away a book as their business card, but even those people who are authors often- times miss out on that chance to give it away.

Your book is such a powerful credibility piece. It is an example of your elite status as an author. So few people ever become authors that when you show yourself as an author, you raise yourself in the eyes of your prospect or contact instantly.

Well, your peers, especially if you are networking in the same groups, the same BNI chapters or the same chamber groups that you have been for the past two or three years, when you pull your book out, they are in awe of you, and they want to be an author, and they can't believe you're an author. They don't understand how suddenly you could be just their friend or the person they see once a month, and now you're this person on a pedestal that has written a book because it's such a rare thing to be an author.

They are excited to get the book, and again, it's a gift to them from you, and they are never going to forget that. They're going to go home and read it and again, with the stickiness of the book, they will see it on a regular basis. They're going to be telling other people about it, "Hey, I just got this book today."

Everett attended a networking event about six years

ago. When a gentleman introduced himself to Everett, he handed Everett a free copy of his book instead of his business card. Everett was completely blown away. In fact, Everett started immediately asking questions about how he became an author, what it was like to be an author and other such questions.

Now, the book itself wasn't of interest to Everett at all. Quite frankly, it was a book of ethnic poetry that Everett just really wasn't excited to go read, but that really didn't matter at all. What did matter was that Everett was incredibly impressed by this individual, impressed by the fact that he was an author first and impressed by the gift of a free book.

That book still wanders around Everett's office as Everett moves it about, but he just can't bring himself to throw it away even though he never intends to read it.

Now if you're going to use your book as a business card, you might as well go the extra mile and sign it for them too. Everyone is always touched and impressed that someone has signed a book. We have had people approach us with copies of our books and ask us to sign it even though we don't really always understand why.

Go ahead and sign the book for the person that you're giving it to, and you might as well go ahead and put your phone number or email address in there while you are signing it. This way, this person can get a hold of you when they want to engage with you for a business or otherwise.

4 - THE PERFECT GIFT

One of the simplest ways to make money with your book is to merely give it away. You can give this away to friends, families, business associates, prospects, or anyone else that you think could benefit from the message and the information that you have to share. This will do some things immediately.

First, it immediately puts that person in a position where they are grateful for the gift. You have given them something that, to you, may only cost a few dollars but, to them, is perceived at costing perhaps $15 to $20. Not only that, there's also the perception that what is in a book is always more valuable than the cover price.

Many people talk about the value of one idea; what could one idea do in your life or in your business. When you give somebody a book, there's always that potential that in that book will be some nugget, some piece of information that will ultimately be priceless to them. Therefore, this gift you've given them could ultimately be priceless.

The other thing that a book will do for you when you give it to somebody is it helps to position you not only as an author but as an expert in your space; they will regard you more highly. For some people, it may be that this gift is the first time they knew that you were an author. Therefore, this is a nice and subtle way to say it without saying, "Hey, I'm an author."

Now once they are holding your book, of course they may find that they want to engage with you based upon the content of that book; they may decide that they want to do business with you, or they may instead refer others to you. They may be talking to a friend and say, "Hey, I need to introduce you to my friend Jenn, who is this great author," and business may flow from there.

Also, the person that you give the book to may decide to share the book with others. They may say, "This is a great book; you need to get it." Or they may turn around and give it to somebody else. A book really can be the gift that keeps on giving, so to speak.

Now another advantage to giving your book away occurs if you happen to have put a lead capture mechanism in your book. A lead capture mechanism is simply an opportunity for somebody to take some sort of action in your book to get bonus material or other resources from you. This could be as simple as having them email an email address, call a phone number, or visit a website; it could also be scanning a Quick Response code or using their phone to text.

If you've put some sort of lead capture mechanism in your book, then the more books you give away, the more chance you have for people to join your list, so that you can market to them for follow-up sales.

5 - GETTING PAST THE GATEKEEPER

A lot of times it's hard to get past the gatekeeper, especially when you're in a business where you need to get past lawyers, doctors, or any other high-profile person.

You must get past the front desk or past the gatekeeper to talk to the person who makes the decisions. One really good way to do this is to get a copy of your book in front of them.

Once you get your book on Amazon, then you can purchase your book from Amazon.com and mark it as a gift. When you are marking it as a gift, you can ship it to your potential client, and you can send it to their home address, if you can get that, or their office address. It's free shipping if you have Amazon Prime.

Now when you are marking it as Gift Wrap from Amazon, you also want to add a personal card. This also is something you can do with Amazon; you can add a personal statement or a personal note along with the book, and one good thing to do with that is to have a YouTube link in your personal message.

The YouTube video you create for someone can be a private video to them, and they can go to that link on YouTube and view your video that says something in the manner of, "Hello this is my book you have holding in your hand, and I have an idea on how you can grow your business." Then you can detail the benefits of your service and why they should buy from you.

This will give you position and authority. It looks great; it's wrapped in paper. Amazon really does a good job with their gift wrapping.

When you do this, make sure that you not only selected it as a gift, but go ahead and pay the extra few bucks to have Amazon gift wrap it for you. They wrap it up very nicely. This way, even if the secretary opens the box, they'll be confronted with a wrapped gift. Most executives frown upon having their receptionists open up their private communications when they come wrapped as gifts. Therefore, the secretary or receptionist is likely to pass this gift on still wrapped to the prospect.

That way, the prospect, and only the prospect, initially opens it to discover your personal note as well as your book and maybe a link to your online video or other greeting.

This happens to be one strategy employed by highly successful internet marketer Mike Koenigs. He will select a very small group of people that he wishes to get his book in front of, and he will go ahead and use Amazon's Gift Wrap feature to place a gift-wrapped book in front of these prospects. He has had great results with this, particularly when he also provides a link to a brief video that he's placed on YouTube for this individual.

When you think about it, what other way can you, for literally the cost of the book and a few dollars for wrapping, get not just your book but also your message and your face in front of a high value prospect, especially one that you never could have gotten in front of before because of their gatekeeper. This truly is a silver bullet to get in front of those high value prospects.

As a side note, there is a story floating around about Nido Qubein, a famous author and businessmen. As the story goes, he took the time to write an entire book to get in front of five particular prospects. He picked five very high value prospects that were CEOs of large companies. He wrote and published the book and had it sent to each of these people with the book specifically giving attention to those five people's challenges, their successes and more. As we understand it, he was able to engage with three or more of those five prospects. Now THAT is way to leverage a book!

6 - GET SPEAKING GIGS

One of the most effective ways to make money with your book is to leverage your book for speaking engagements. You can do this several different ways.

Locally, you can use your book to get speaking engagements at nonprofit events and at service organizations. It's often very easy to lend an opportunity to speak in front of rotary clubs, BNI groups and for local nonprofits if you have a book.

We've spoken before on how authors really a rare thing are, and these organizations rarely get calls from people who are authors, let alone Amazon Bestselling authors.

Getting a speaking engagement is often just as simple as finding who the proper contact person is at the target organization, making a phone call and introducing yourself as the author of an Amazon Bestselling book, etc. Very often, they will bend over backwards to find a time for you to come and speak to their group, provided that your topic is useful to them.

In an environment where you are not able to sell, it's very important for you to recognize that people are likely to come up afterward and want to get more information from you. If you strategically plant in your talk statements about the clients that you work with and the things you do with clients, then you will be planting in the mind of your listener the fact that you work with clients and that you help them with these areas.

There will almost definitely be people in your audience that will come up to you afterwards and ask to do business with you or at least explore that possibility. When this occurs, understand that it is your book that helped get you there, and it is your book that is helping you make money in this circumstance.

But there is also a way to make money on your book even though you can't sell your book at an event like this.

One of our clients, when speaking to rotary groups, gives the rotary group the option of either allowing him to sell his book while donating a portion of the proceeds to the organization, or he will give them a certain number of copies of the book, to make sure that each person who is in attendance gets a copy of the book.

This is an incredibly powerful tool that we'll go into in further detail in chapter 16. But just understand that having a book position you as a desired speaker and then positions you with authority when you do those speeches.

As you know the subtitle of this book is *The Top 20 Ways to Make Money on Your Book (even if you haven't written it yet)*. We want you potential speakers, current speakers, and those professionals out there who speak all the time without a book of your own to know that with a book, you can get so many more speaking gigs and speaking engagements. With a book, you have that leverage to position yourself as more of an expert speaker or more of an authority to speak on the certain subject.

It's very important for you to recognize that once you are an author, Amazon bestseller or not, you may now command higher fees as a speaker. Not only are you more likely to be selected for speaking opportunities, but you're more likely to get higher fees as a result.

One of our clients, who we are not at leisure to disclose, saw his speaking income increase 600% following the publishing and launch of his Amazon bestselling book. He found that organizations were far more likely to engage him as a speaker, and he also found that he was able to significantly increase his fees.

This curve of increasing fees that he is on, will continue as well because as he gets more and more opportunities, he is able to be more and more selective. He can raise his fees because he knows that he will have enough speaking opportunities, even with a substantially higher fee.

One great story on how to leverage a book for speaking engagements comes from one of our mentors, Ed Rush. Ed wrote a book called *Turning Clicks into Profits*, he wrote this book particularly with the legal industry in mind. He and his team then called local bar associations and informed them as part of their book launch that they were on a speaking tour and offered to come and speak to their organizations.

The bar associations were thrilled to have an author come, teach their people about how to market their law firms online, but they were concerned that Ed might try to sell something, which they simply don't allow in their bar association meetings. Ed quickly assured them that not only would they not be selling anything at the event, but that they would like to go ahead and give a copy of the book to every person in attendance. Each of the local bar chapters were ecstatic over this offer.

When Ed arrived at the event, he gave everybody a book which, of course, made everybody very happy and pleased. He then went ahead and spoke in detail about how they could generate more business by marketing their practices effectively online. During the conversation, he dropped statements like, "What we do with our clients is…" and "When you meet with us…" throughout his presentation.

Inevitably, he had at least a handful of the people in attendance approaching him immediately after the meeting to seek his company's assistance in marketing their business. This was so effective that the attorneys would sometimes get in competition with each other. They would try to engage Ed's firm exclusively to exclude any of the other people in attendance from working with him in their marketing.

7 - BACK OF ROOM SALES

One of the best and easiest ways to make money with your book is to sell it at the back of a room or on a table whenever you have the opportunity to speak at an event.

This is great on multiple levels. One great reason is because when you are speaking at an event, there will be those people who want to go deeper into your content and want to get more of your information.

Having your book for sale at the back of the room gives them an opportunity to dive deeper into your information and to compensate you immediately for that information. However, having the book for sale at the back of the room also does something advantageous for you at the front of the room, and that is this: people have heard that you are an author, but now they are seeing your books, and those books at the back of the room help to give you greater authority at the front of the room.

Think about when you have gone to a large event and an author has spoken. Typically, they have books at the back for sale. So if you can do the same thing, it just positions you in the same way as these famous authors or speakers.

Make the most of your book sales by putting them on display at the back of the room. Not only will this attract potential buyers, but it also allows you to interact with your fans through book signings. You can either sign books at the table set up for you or as customers purchase them. Don't miss out on this chance to engage with your audience and boost book sales.

Naturally, you're going to want to explore this opportunity with the hosts of the event to make sure that you're good to do this. But often, they will want to see you do that because it just adds that much more credibility to their event because they have a published author who is having a book signing right at their event.

Now, if you're going to have your books for sale at the back of the room, it really is critical that it's not you selling the books at the back of the room. You really need to have somebody there to do that for you, whether it's somebody from your office, somebody who is a volunteer at the event, etc. It really is important that it's not you back there selling the book.

Simply think back again to those times when you have been at large events where there were authors selling books. You never see a big author or a famous author, selling his own book. Therefore, you don't want to be there selling your own book either. It takes away some of that positioning and authority that you've worked so hard to establish.

Also, there are often things that are going to happen at the front of the room that are far more valuable than what may happen at the back. When you walk off stage, you may be approached by a high value prospect, and you don't want to have to tell that prospect, "Oh, I'm sorry I can't talk to you because I need to race to the back of the room to sell books for $15 or $20."

We ran into exactly this situation with one of our clients, Frank Leyes. He wrote a terrific book called *The Way of Wealth*, it was an Amazon's bestseller in five categories. Frank speaks to financial consultants and also speaks to potential clients in the financial services industry. When he is approached by someone to have a con- versation, this client may have a million dollars or more that they wish to invest through Frank's company. It doesn't make any sense at all for Frank to put that per- son off to go and sell his books at the back of the room.

Unfortunately, though, when Frank is at an event, he's usually there by himself, and there's nobody else at that event that is able to assist in those back-of-room. Fortunately, we found an elegant solution for Frank.

We researched on Amazon for something that would make a decent box that would be able to show the offer of the book and to collect money on an honor system. What we found was a beautiful cherry wood comment box. The box had a place for him to slip an 8.5x11 piece of paper in the front, it also was a locking box with a slot in the top for people to drop their money.

In Frank's environment, it made sense to use the honor system, and he simply said, "Here's the book; they are $15 a piece or 2 for $20." He left that at the back of the room with a stack of books. Every time he speaks, books disappear, and money shows up in the box, and he's never had any problem.

Now is it possible that someone is going to steal a book or two? Yes. Is that highly likely or is that going to significantly compromise the profitability of that sale? It really isn't, and Frank has used the box on multiple occasions and has never really had any significant problem.

So sell your books at the back of the room whether you have a volunteer or whether you use a nice box, but definitely, sell your books at the back of the room. You can grab the same comment box as Frank right now at http://goo.gl/uurRD8.

8 - YOUR BOOK AS OFFICE DÉCOR

One great way to utilize your book and make money on your book is to use it as office décor. A great place to start is in your office; whether you are a doctor, or you have a reception area in your office, you can set it on the coffee table, or you can put it on the bookcase. You can leave multiple copies out for people if they want to get a copy, and you can have your receptionist offer that to them either for sale or as a gift.

You've certainly walked into lots of offices where you've found a variety of magazines, mostly old issues. Think about how much more powerful it is for someone who's walking into your office to see a copy of your

book sitting on the counter or coffee table for them to peruse. Having the book there and available immediately helps to position you as an authority and expert.

It also may give them an opportunity to thumb through the book and read portions before they ever come to meet you. This is going to have a dramatic effect on the tone of your conversation, particularly if this is the person's first time coming into your office.

We often talk about books as not being a lead-generating strategy, but instead as a conversion strategy. What we mean by this is that a book doesn't often bring you a lead; it doesn't necessarily bring you a name or a new person. But it is a conversion tool in the sense that it helps you convert those people that you meet or that you come in contact with.

Having that book sitting on your coffee table in your reception area not only makes you an expert but gives them a chance to get a feel of you before they ever meet with you. We think; that if you employ this strategy, you will find that your prospects and customers are far more compliant and far more likely to engage with you at a deeper and more profitable level.

Another way to use your book as office décor is to position your book strategically on the bookcase in your office, so that your client can see it. Your client is continuously reminded that they are not just talking to any average person; they are talking to an author and perhaps to an Amazon bestselling author.

Now this is even more powerful if you have done an Amazon bestseller launch and have had your book reprinted with an bestseller seal on the front cover indicating that you are an Amazon bestseller. Alternatively, if you don't have your book reprinted, you can have foil seals or other things made to demonstrate to people that your book was an Amazon bestseller. Whatever you do, make sure that the book is visible in your office.

If you happen to participate in any online interviews or if you ever communicate to people via webcam, make sure that your book shows in the background. Make sure that it is part of the image that people see whenever they talk to you on webcam or if they conduct an online interview with you. Again, this is another way to position yourself in front of people, and they can see you as an expert and authority figure and be far more likely to engage with you and be more profitable when they do.

9 - LET PEOPLE KNOW ABOUT YOUR BOOK

If you want to make money with your book, people have to know about it. One of the worst things that an author can do is write a book, tell a few people about it and then just assume that everyone else knows that they are an author. Pretty soon, any buzz that may have been generated about their book is gone, and people are no longer discussing the book; they may not even remember that the author wrote the book.

We are a big proponent of making people know about your book. You can help to educate them in numerous ways. Some people put a reference to their book on their email signature; other people place the book on their business card. We know people who make sure that they have a plaque or framed picture in their office referencing the book and their bestseller release. Still others may brand their social media with their book.

If you go to either of our LinkedIn profiles, you will certainly see in the first line or two that we are Amazon bestselling authors. In addition, we know people who have changed their Facebook profile page to show a copy of their book and maybe the fact that it is an Amazon bestseller. All these things are very important if you want people to understand that you are an author and to give you the authority and respect that comes with authorship.

Now we share this with you not to tell you that you need to go brag to everybody that you are an author, and we don't want you to focus all your concentration on the fact that you are an author or that you're an Amazon bestselling author. We know that it is challenging, and we know that you don't want people to see you as "tooting your own horn." But you won't make more money with your book if people don't know that you have a book. You won't make more money because you are an author if people don't know you are an author.

Therefore, consistently, let people know that you have a book. Of course, you want to be tactful and not act like you're bragging or that it's the only thing you talk about, but you have accomplished something extraordinary, and you need to take credit for that fact.

Think about this. If you were an Olympic athlete, and you earned a gold medal, would you simply hang it in your closet and never tell anybody about it? We doubt that. Instead, you'll see most Olympic athletes leverage that accomplishment to get writing deals, speaking engagements, commercials, sponsorships and more.

You have accomplished something extraordinary by becoming an author and even more extraordinary if you have become an Amazon bestselling author, and you need to leverage that to the hilt.

Your book will do something profound to you. You cannot write a book and publish it to the world without it having some significant impact upon you. That impact could be, and likely will be, in sales, but it will also likely have an internal impact upon your own mental state. It will affect your posture as you deal with people, and it may have some impact upon your own confidence and perception of self-worth. This is really to be welcomed and embraced.

10 - ELEVATOR SPEECH

It's important when you are talking to others about what you do that you have a specific elevator speech or a pitch that includes that you are a bestseller on Amazon or that you have written a book that is available on Amazon. You need to lever- age the branding and make sure that everyone knows you are on Amazon. By telling them in your elevator speech that you have a book and that you're a bestselling author, this leads to more conversation about what your book is about, and it opens up the conversation, instead of just stating your profession and not going any further from there.

This goes back to what we discussed in chapter 9 where we said that you need to let people know about your book. Letting people know in your elevator speech or 60-second commercial that you are an author immediately positions you as an expert.

You'll find that it will greatly surprise the prospect to whom you're speaking to, because authorship is so rare.

For example, Everett was recently flying home from a client's event in Virginia and was sitting on the air- plane next to an individual who was a very prominent businessman in Everett's hometown. The gentleman had recently sold his business, was retired and "living the high life."

When he asked Everett what he did, Everett simply said, "Well, I'm an Amazon bestselling author, and I assist my clients in positioning themselves as experts in their

industries through authorship, podcasts and more." This individual, who was probably in his late 60s and very wealthy, turned to Everett and said, "You know, I don't think I've ever met an author." The conversation from there was quite different than any other casual conversation that two people would most likely have after meeting on an airplane.

Including your book in your elevator speech is perhaps one of the best ways that you can leverage your accomplishment and let people know about your book. Again, this will help you convert that person because they are far more interested in you now that they have found that you are an author, and you will find more conversations leading to future businesses as a result.

11- PRESS RELEASE

Another way to let people know about your book is by creating an online press release. Along with the press releases, you can submit an article or blog to publications in your local area, or you can send them for distribution throughout the country. Press releases are a great way to get the message out and to really leverage what your book is about and who you are. Having your press release in a national publication is also a great way to leverage yourself because you can then say, "As seen in the Wall Street Journal" or "As seen on CNN.com" or any other known website. You want to make sure that you get a press release written. The press release can be about yourself as a bestseller, or it can just be simply about your book.

There are a number of online tools that are very effective at distributing press releases throughout the world. The beauty of these tools is that you can simply create one press release and watch it be distributed to literally hundreds, if not thousands, of different media sources. The more you do this, naturally, the more likely it is that your book or your information will be picked up and featured by a media outlet.

Furthermore, the more your information is featured by a media outlet, the more likely it is you may be called to be interviewed for a radio or a television appearance or to simply appear in print or online media. These tools can range from $30 to $500 per press release, depending upon the features that you desire. While I am sure some- one would be happy to educate us on why we should spend $500 for the press release, we have been happy with less expensive offerings!

Here are a few press release sites:

Release Wire: Releasewire.com

Business Wire: Businesswire.com

PR Reach: Prreach.com

PR Web: Prweb.com

Following a press release, make sure to log in to the press release platform after a couple of days to see where your press release has been featured. At this time, you could consider utilizing the fact that your information has been featured on those sources while positioning yourself as an author or your book. As mentioned above, this is a great way to develop the "as seen on" links and logos for your website, for your speaking one sheet, and other collateral.

One of our clients is a financial planner, and he used a company out there called *Help a Reporter*. With this website, you can submit articles or press releases for reporters to use. If they use your article or press release in their news publications, they will contact you. Help a Reporter has a portal you can log into to make sure you know which publications your article is featured in."

Our client now has on his website, "As seen in the Wall Street Journal, Money News, the local tribune, Newsmax.com, and the Enterprise." There are so many different publications that he's been in simply by helping a reporter at Helpareporter.com.

12 - SELLING AT ONLINE BOOKSTORES

So far, we've given you numerous ways to make money for your book, without even discussing some of the most obvious ones. When people first think of becoming an author, the traditional way to make money is to sell your book in bookstores – online or otherwise.

> **"I always think of Jack Canfield from The Secret. He talks about how he only needs to sell 1 million copies to the readers of the National Enquirer at a dollar apiece to make a million dollars."**
> **- Jenn Foster**

One of the beautiful things about technology today is it allows self-publishing authors to place their books almost anywhere online. The Kindle Direct Publishing tool allows people to create their book and place it for sale on Amazon, but there are other tools that will allow you to place your book for sale at numerous online platforms.

Ingram Spark, Draft2Digital and Book Baby are great self-publishing tools. If you upload your book to one of these sites, you'll have the option to have your book for sale on multiple online book shops like: iBooks, Amazon Kindle, Nook, Kobo, and about forty other online bookstores.

If you're going to write a book, you naturally want to sell as many copies as possible. If you want to sell as many copies as possible, it certainly makes sense to have your book for sale in as many outlets as possible. This is where tools like IngramSpark and others really shine because not only will your book be for sale at Amazon, but it will also be for sale at Barnes & Noble and multiple other large and small retail stores online, including libraries.

This is a good time for a brief discussion about the online pricing of your book. Many people understandably want to make as much money per sale as possible and therefore, want to place their book at the highest price that they believe they can reasonably sell it at.

We completely understand this; we would certainly prefer to make $10 in profit per book rather than $5 per profit. But you need to consider the value of your information, and the likelihood that you're going to convert a reader into a follow-on sale or a high- er-end sale. Mike Koenigs, for instance, will place many of his books on Amazon at the cheapest price he can possibly select in the system.

Mike recognizes that it would be very shortsighted of him to sell his book for $20 even though it may merit that price. He recognizes that it is far more valuable for as many people as possible to get his book, so that they can join his list and be presented follow-up purchase opportunities worth far more than any royalty he would make from any book.

This type of pricing decision applies not just to your paperback books but also to your Kindle books or Nook, for that matter if you use those platforms. You may need to consider whether or not you are better off using a very inexpensive price for your book in order to get as many copies as possible out there rather than selecting a higher price to generate a higher royalty.

You need to consider your own industry and what your other follow-up opportunities are to engage. If the only way you must make money from your book is royalties, then set the fees accordingly. However, if you have opportunities for people to engage with you at a much higher price point through other opportunities, then price the book at a lower level and get more copies out.

We do understand that there is also a positioning value to price. We have worked with clients who have indicated that they have to have a decent price on the book for the book to be considered a serious book. We understand this. We also understand that there are certain industries where a high price point on a book is not only expected but essentially is demanded. Certain legal documents and reference books come to mind.

The Book on Better Roads by Blair Barnhardt is one example, where he priced his book at $50 because of the industry in which he was selling the book. This, of course, gave a certain level of credibility to the book. However, it also gave him the opportunity to significantly discount the book if he chose to, whether at live events or in online promotions. Whatever you do, consider your pricing carefully.

13 - SELLING ON YOUR WEBSITE

Now that you have your book, and you are a bestseller on Amazon; you need to have a website to feature your book. You can have a website that features you as an author and your book. To do that, you want to have a website that includes your chapter titles, a bio page (or "about the author" as it could be called), and a contact page with information on how they can best con- tact you. You might want to include a gallery page or an event page for your speaking engagements and pictures from events that you've done, and then of course, the "Buy Now" button, or a way for visitors to buy the book on your website with a simple checkout.

You should post a link to Amazon with your affiliate link to direct people to your book. If you are giving your e-book away for free or posting it for sale on Amazon, you can have either one of those links on your website as well.

Remember that featuring your book for sale on your website is as much a positioning and conversion tool as it is an actual revenue generator. Even if people fail to buy the book from your website, the fact that they've seen it there is one more opportunity for your prospect to understand that you are an author and perhaps a best-selling author.

If you put your book for sale on your corporate web-site, for instance, don't be upset if you don't sell a lot of copies. Understand that the book is accomplishing far more for you by just being present there than it may be in any actual royalty sales.

As for a mechanism for selling your book, one of the simplest ways to do it is simply to link directly to Amazon for the sale. We are big fans of keeping people out of the fulfillment industry. You have something that you are really good at, and it probably isn't boxing and shipping books. For this reason, go ahead and leverage Amazon or other online sources for the actual sale and fulfillment. Yes, they will charge a small premium for the service, but it is well worth it if it keeps you working in your area of unique giftedness.

As far as which online tools you may utilize, they are numerous, and they are changing all the time. While simply redirecting people to Amazon is a very simple method, there are others out there.

There is also a strategy that may encourage you to fulfill your books in house. If you wish to put some sort of promotional item, personal note, or other gift with your books when people buy them, then it may be ap- propriate to go ahead and fulfill those books at your own business. However, even if you wish to give a gift, note, or other item with your book, there are fulfillment services out there that can put custom attachments with your book. Consider those.

14 - USING YOUR BOOK AT A TRADE SHOW

If you couldn't tell already, we are great proponents of making sure that your book gets in as many hands as possible. A trade

show is often a terrific environment to make that happen. We have seen clients use their books as giveaways at trade shows to those people who visit their booths. We have seen people sell books at their trade show booths, and we have seen people use them as raffle prizes and other incentives at their booths.

How you use your book at a trade show really depends upon the nature of your business and what other types of things you are trying to accomplish at the trade show. Certainly, if you are an author and have an Amazon Bestselling book, it makes sense for your trade show prospects to understand this. We recommend that you include images of your book in your signage and have physical copies of your book available for sale or to simply give away. This just makes sense.

Remember that your book is a conversion tool and will help to convert prospects. Therefore, people walk- ing up to your booth at a trade show need to see the book and understand that you are an author. If this occurs, they are far more likely to engage with you.

Keep in mind that you may be the only booth at a trade show that features an author and a bestselling book. This is unique and powerful, particularly when people are walking around, looking at endless rows of booths that all start to fade into one another. Your book is one way for your booth to stand out.

A very powerful way to make money with your book at a trade show is to arrange to have free copies of your book given away in the goodie bags that are commonly given to people when they attend a trade show. If you can get a copy of your book into each of the attendees' hands, perhaps with some note or effort or other reference to your trade show booth, then you will go a long way to bringing more traffic to your booth and helping you convert that traffic more readily.

We know this can seem expensive when you consider that you are probably going to spend $2 or $4 per copy on your book but think about how much money you al- ready spend per lead at your booth. Many people are spending this much money or more on key chains and other things that they may give away. In this case, you are giving away something of a far greater perceived value than anyone else, and this is also something that won't be thrown away.

Let's face it, most people gather all the freebies they can at a trade show but turn around and throw essentially all of it away. People have a hard time throwing away books because they have such high perceived value. Now, on a side note, it's critical that your book not look like a flyer or an advertisement. Your book needs to look like a legitimate book that people would find for sale in a bookstore. Otherwise, people will indeed throw it away.

For this reason, we are not great fans of featuring a business logo or something of that nature on the cover of a book. We recognize that there is a place for such a logo, but if you walk through a bookstore, you'll find that very few books feature a logo or any other promo- tional look. Your book needs to look serious to be taken seriously, unless, of course, your brand is a very playful one, and you don't want to be taken seriously.

If you don't want to give thousands of books away to every person visiting a trade show, another option would be to give five to ten copies of your book to the host of the trade show to give as a drawing or giveaway. Of course, always have a mention of your trade booth number when they are giving your books away.

Most trade shows do drawings throughout the show and give away different items. You could also give away something with your book that goes along with your product or service.

Let's say you have written an Amazon Bestselling book on how to use Facebook as a marketing tool. Imagine how effective it could be if you got the event host to give away a free one-hour consultation with the author of the bestselling book on marketing with Facebook. This is a very effective strategy, and it helps to advertise you as a Facebook expert to all the attendees at the trade show. It also helps to position you as somebody in demand since it will be seen that some lucky winner is going to get an hour consultation with you wherein you will give them free advice about generating more business online.

15 - YOUR BOOK AS AN ESCALATION STRATEGY

Probably the most profitable way to utilize your book to make money is as part of an escalation strategy. A typical escalation strategy in the online world often starts by giving away something for free or selling something very inexpensively and then, over time, escalating sales into larger, more expensive products and services. We call this an *escalation strategy*, and it is highly effective in the online world. A book can be a very powerful portion of an escalation strategy.

Everett and Jenn are members of several mastermind groups. One of our mastermind groups decided to collectively co-author a book called *There's Money in This Book: 17 Secrets From A Marketing Mastermind*. Each author in the book put a specific call to action at the end of each chapter designed to offer the reader some other free resource. The purpose of this call to action is really to incentivize the reader to get on a list with each one of the authors in the book.

Everett, for instance, offered a "value of a client calculator" to those people who would send in their email address. This is really the opening salvo in an escalation strategy. Once somebody is on a list, further offers can be made for more substantial and expensive products and tools.

In the case of *There's Money in This Book*, each author has the opportunity to take the reader and walk them into significant offerings, whether it be more expensive products or whether it be one-on-one services or even coaching. Ultimately, this one book could result in many,

many thousands of dollars in revenue simply because somebody read a book and decided to ask for more information.

Therefore, we want to emphasize the importance of having some sort of lead capture in your book. That lead capture should be there along with some sort of incentive or ethical bribe, so that people will text or email in order to get some other resource information from you. Then you'll have the opportunity to "drip market" to that person for other sales opportunities and more.

Remember that an escalation strategy like this doesn't only have to apply online, and it doesn't only have to involve lead capture in your book. We've discussed the book as your 100-page flyer or as your thick business card, and the book is naturally part of your escalation strategy. Your book should be one of the first things that you give to prospects, and it will likely be the tool that helps you leverage greater and greater fees and make it more likely for that person to do business with you going forward.

Let's take a look at how Mike Koenigs uses a book specifically in his escalation strategy. Mike makes sure to give as many books away as possible and to sell them as cheaply as possible to get books into as many people's hands as possible. In each book, he has opportunities for people to request more information and to ultimately get on a list for that information. From that list, Mike will market the opportunity for people to buy products. They could be as inexpensive as $500 or as expensive as $5,000.

He will also utilize that list in order to encourage people's attendance at an event that people may pay

$100 to attend. But when he gets people at the event, he will have several substantial product offerings ranging in price from $2,000 to $10,000. He may even offer a personal mastermind or coaching program for $20,000 or more.

Therefore, this simple book that he has given away or sold for very little may help to bring him a prospect that, over time, could engage in $50,000 or more in sales over the next several years. We hope you can see how this book is a part of a serious opportunity for greater sales.

Now this can also be true if you are a doctor, attorney, accountant, or other business professional or owner. Getting a book into someone's hand can simply be the opening step into doing further business with them. Depending on the business you are in, your book could be the beginning of hundreds of dollars in sales or hundreds of thousands of dollars in sales. It just depends upon your industry and how you use it.

16 - FREE GIVEAWAY

Using your book in a giveaway or handing it out for free is a great way to get more books into more hands, and that's what we've

been talking about in this book so far. Often time for Christmas, a local realtor in our area will have a huge movie event where he'll invite all of his clients to a movie. Having a book in the goodie bags would give him so much leverage and authority if he was an author, but unfortunately, he has not written a book.

That many people getting your book when they are going to the movie, free like that, is not going to end up in the garbage like we talked about before. At any live event that you do, you should have a free giveaway for each person there or have a special drawing for the give-away of your book. Another way is if you are doing a drawing or giveaway to have that book signed for that specific person. It gives you a little bit more authority as an expert if you sign the copy to them.

Another thing to do if it's a big event like the real estate movie would be to sponsor the event. Your company could give away a book and sponsor that movie event, and again signing the book over to the person who wins the drawing.

Depending on what industry you are in, you will find different opportunities to give away your books. One of our friends has written an Amazon Bestselling book on decorating with balloons. It would certainly make sense for her to give away that book at a craft show or at an event planners conference. Doing so would give her more and more opportunities to engage with people for further business.

If your book happens to be on dog training, then it would be profitable for you to give away that book at dog shows or events around the whole pet industry. You need to look for specific opportunities to give away your book at events. Keep in mind, again, that while many other free giveaways at events will get thrown away, your book, most likely, will not get thrown away.

In fact, you'll probably find that your book will be wandering around someone's desk a couple years from now simply because they couldn't bring themselves to throw it away. This will often be a great branding reminder as people will continually be reminded of you and your business. Ultimately, some of those people will pick up the book and call you, and that, of course, is what we want to see happen.

Even if they don't call you right away, you are still benefiting from the additional positioning and exposure of people seeing your book. Consider for a moment how much money is spent by people giving away branded pens in goodie bags and at events. Some serious money is spent that way. How much more effective and powerful is a book that features you, your message, and maybe also your image?

That is far more effective and will have much greater legs than almost any other thing that could be given away in someone's goodie bag.

17 - EVENT CONTEST WHEN SPEAKING OR PRESENTING

A friend of ours, Paul Colligan, is a public speaker and an expert at podcasting, video marketing, and other online marketing. One of his favorite strategies when speaking is to run a contest with his book during a live event. What he will do is stand up on stage and announce a contest for his book.

He will tell people that there are books for sale at the back of the room or that will be handed out by volunteers in the room, but he will make sure to include some money in those books, maybe a $20 bill, a $50 bill or a $100 bill.

Of course, you could also do the same thing with some other prize, maybe a consulting session with you, some other product from your business, etc.

One great strategy is to employ some sort of list building tool while speaking from the stage and to then incentivize people to join that list. We have a tool that we call the "Crowd Grabber" in a specific software system, it allows people to text in to receive more information, or to send an email or even a voicemail to get on your list and get further resources from you.

If you want to run a contest from the stage, take a stack of your books and give them to a volunteer at the back of the room, place some money in some of the books. Depending upon how generous you are, you might include some $5 bills, $20 bills, 50s, or even 100s.

Now while on stage, tell people that you will give a free copy of your book to anybody who texts into your list. Then have them hold up their phones when they've done so, and a volunteer will bring them a free copy of the book. Then, of course, tell people that there's money in some of these books as well and that some people may win $50 or $100. Then watch what happens.

What you will see is countless people racing to text in to get on your list and raising their phones in the air. This, of course, reinforces to everyone who hasn't done it yet that they should do it, and soon you'll have a crowd full of people standing up with their phones in the air, in order to get the free book and the chance at some free money. This is a terrific way to get people on to your list, so that you can market to them and communicate with them later.

Of course, you need to make sure that you have enough books for your audience. You could make a scarcity play and limit the number of books that are available and announce that from the stage. But remember, your goal is to get books in as many hands as possible and to get as many people on your list as possible. Therefore, we recommend playing it safe and making sure to have a copy for each person, even though not everyone will take a book. It is better to have some leftover books than to lose the opportunity to put your book in someone's hands.

Keep in mind the varied benefits of employing such a strategy. First, there is the value of a gift. People will appreciate the generosity you are showing them by giving away a book. Remember also that a book is worth far more than the paper it's printed on, and people understand this. You'll also benefit from the greater exposure of having as many books as possible in as many hands as possible.

You will also be reinforcing the fact that you are an author, and you'll also be giving each person an opportunity to hold a physical copy of your book in their hands. We can't overstate the value of people physically holding that book. The tactile experience of holding the book just continues to build your authority and your position as an expert.

Also, know your book may be the only book that they leave the event with. Think of how powerful that will be if the only thing they take home from that event, or if the only book they take home, happens to be yours. We believe that this strategy is a win on multiple levels.

We mentioned that there are multiple ways to run this type of a contest. First, you can incentivize the contest in numerous ways. In addition to giving away money, you might instead give away a consultation or some other product that comes from your business. You also may consider numerous different tools to employ when conducting this strategy.

Our favorite tool to use is one we mentioned prior in this chapter, called Instant Customer and the "Crowd Grabber" feature within Instant Customer. This allows people to text in to get on to your list, but they can also employ email, a QR code, a voicemail, or lead capture on a website to join the list. We have found this tool to be very effective.

Darren Hardy, the publisher of SUCCESS magazine, employs this strategy when speaking at live events and has gathered information from as much as 90% of an audience. We've employed this strategy with many of our clients. The first time Frank Leyes used this strategy, he got information from 60% of the audience. This is a very effective strategy, and a great way for you to make money with your book by giving it away.

18 - NEW AND BETTER OPPORTUNITIES

We've discussed a book as part of an escalation strategy previously. But there is a different kind of escalation strategy that can occur in your business because of a book. With your newfound status as an author comes a level of credibility that is unparalleled in the business world. As an author, you are instantly seen as an expert and an authority in your industry.

As a result, additional opportunities are going to come to you. Ultimately, this is perhaps one of the most profound ways that you can make money with your book, but you won't do it through book sales so much as what the book will do to you.

When Everett wrote his first book, *The Video Tractor Beam*, he chose to write it on video marketing because it was something that his business was engaging in. Ultimately however, he wrote the book mostly as a proof of concept for the method of writing and launching the book.

People immediately started to see Everett as an expert in video creation, production, and marketing. This wasn't the reason Everett published the book, but the outcome was inevitable. As a result, people started to approach Everett not just to get their videos produced and marketed but also to learn more from him and how to produce those videos.

As a result, Everett has found himself now as a consultant to other people who are working in the video marketing world. This was a completely unexpected result of publishing the book. In retrospect, however, it was a completely predictable result.

When you publish a book, it will change your business and in many ways. Not only will it allow you the opportunity to do consulting, as it did for Everett, but it also may provide you opportunities to do done-for-you services for other professionals. People may approach you to come alongside them to do similar projects that you've written about. Ultimately, this will vary depending upon your industry. But you need to be open to the opportunities that may come about as a result.

After publishing his own book, Everett was approached by a friend who was writing a book about marriage, called *The Resurrection Marriage*. He asked Everett to help him complete this book, get it on Amazon and do an Amazon launch. Everett did exactly that, and a couple months later, his friend had an Amazon #1 Bestselling Book on his hands. Everett now has a thriving publishing business helping other experts get their message to the world through books. Jenn also has developed a successful publishing business. As of the writing of this book, Jenn has had more than 6 such bestsellers between her and her clients. Everett is currently launching his 14th.

In addition, publishing a book may also provide you the opportunity to create certification programs and other products around your book.

Because of the book that Jenn published with Dan Kennedy, she received a phone call out of the blue, in the voicemail it simply said, "Help, I need you right now. I've read your chapter three times, and I was up till 1:00 in the morning, and I really need to talk to you. I have a marketing firm in Idaho, and I really would like to partner with you, so that you do our work for us. It seems you know more about doing this type of service than we do. Please call me as soon as possible."

This voicemail led to her working with this individual and this company to do a white label program and actually do the work for his firm in Idaho. Other ways you can leverage on done-for-you services would be someone reading your book and understanding that you do this service, not just talk about how to do it. You do it as in you are a Facebook marketer or a video marketer, or you do consult on your own, and you do the actual physical work for them, or your firm or your company does it for them.

Because of your book, you will get more jobs and more projects to work on because you have that expert and authority by being an author and a bestseller on Amazon.

It's completely natural and predictable that people will be calling you because of your book in order to do services for them. An additional way for you to leverage this; however, is to offer a certification program related to your book topic.

So, for example, if you have written a book regarding training horses, some people will likely call you and be interested in paying you to help train their horses or pay you as a consultant to give them advice about how to train their horses. Ultimately, however, it is possible for you to create a certification program wherein other people will be certified in your method of training horses.

This can have a dramatic impact upon your income level as people may pay not only to get the training, but they may also pay an ongoing licensing fee to utilize your name or brand in their own advertising. Ultimately, it's possible to even create a franchise situation, all built around the brand that you've created around your name and your book.

It is important for you to recognize that with your book; the sky really is the limit. Yes, you can utilize your book simply to generate money from the royalties, but you can generate money in so many other ways from your book.

19 - MEDIA ATTENTION

To attract a lot of media attention with your book, you'll want to get the most exposure you can. The first thing we would suggest is setting up a book signing party and release date, and when you do that, you'll want to create a Facebook event and let everyone know. You can use different press releases, local publications, small newspapers, Chamber of Commerce, involve your local BNI chapter, any other networking group that you have, and tell everyone about your book signing party.

The next thing to do after you set the date and get your Facebook event set up is to get the local radio and TV stations involved and let them know you are having a book signing event. A lot of times, they'll come for free just to have more information or more things in the community.

The other thing you can do with the press releases about your book signing party is Helpareporter.com. On this site you can submit your press release, and they can put it on different publications online; this is also free or for a small charge.

One of the beautiful things about Helpareporter.com is that this is a clearinghouse for experts and reporters to come together to share information. A reporter who happens to be working on a news, television, or radio article or report, often will need to seek sources to discuss current events or some other topic of interest. One of their resources is this website, Helpareporter.com. Once there, the reporters can browse experts in that clearinghouse and reach out to them to include them in an interview or other story. This really is a great way for you to help get your word out because you can often include a URL or other piece of information in your interview or article, and this will undoubtedly drive traffic to your websites and also increase your notoriety.

When approaching local media outlets, make sure to

position yourself as an expert and author. Whether or not you have already launched your book, you are already the author of a book, and this is very important. The people at the media outlets are far more likely to pay attention to you and give you credence if you reference the fact that you are an author.

If you are already an Amazon bestselling author, make sure to reference this, too. Simply describe yourself as the Amazon bestselling author of book X and let them know that you are having a book signing and launch party. Give them the date and location and invite them to attend.

You may also give them a quick blurb about your book and really what it is that you are attempting to accomplish through your book. If this is a cause that the representative of the media outlet can get behind, you may find them helping to support your launch in additional ways. Besides coming to your book signing party, they may feature you in community news publications, invite you to appear on their radio or TV show, write an article around you and your book launch, etc.

Brendon Burchard likes to use this phrase: "People support what they create." Keep this phrase in mind whenever you contact media outlets. Approach them as potential partners in getting your message out. Also let them participate in creation with you if they are so inclined. One way to approach outlets is to simply say something along the lines of the following:

"My name is Everett O'Keefe, and I am the author of the Amazon bestselling book, The Video Tractor

Beam. I'm currently in the process of launching my second book, which is designed to help people leverage publishing to improve their business. Do you have many business clients in your listenership, and is this something that you think your listenership might be interested in? If so, maybe we can create something great together."

There really is no end to the possibilities with local media outlets. Your radio and television shows are constantly looking for content to feature. Because of the nature of these industries, there is a constant turnover of personalities and experts, and therefore a constant need for new ones. In addition, these outlets are always trying to one up each other, and they may see you as a point of distinction for their station, particularly if you are a bestselling author.

You may be able to leverage local media outlets for a regular appearance, a regular column in a newspaper, etc. Whatever you do, always try to work into your presentation, article, or interview something that will direct people to your website and build your list. Sending people to a website where they can opt in for additional resources is always good but giving people the opportunity to text in to join your list (the Crowd Grabber we discussed earlier) is usually your best bet.

Keep in mind that some media outlets will not want you to do this. You need to decide if it will be better for you to get permission in advance or to ask for forgiveness later. Naturally, you do not wish to burn any bridges, so we think that seeking permission in advance is typically the best route.

Now that you have your book signing party date set, you need to plan your book signing party. Make sure that you have an idea of how many people will be coming to your event. You can have your event at a local hair salon, a local restaurant, or any type of office or building that closely relates to your business or field, somewhere that you can host 50 to 100 people or more.

When you know how many people will be coming, you'll want to make sure you have enough books there. You want to make sure that you preorder your books from Kindle Direct Publishing or IngramSpark; you'll have printed books ready to sign. You'll also want to have your Crowd Grabber campaign ready with a tablet, so that people that come to your event in your book release party and will be able to sign in to win something.

You can make it fun; they can put in their name and email with the tablet or computer when they come in. Then throughout the hour or two hours of your party, you can do raffles, you can select random winners. You don't even have to buy the door prizes. Have all the prizes be sponsored donations that are given to you. This way you can feature local businesses in your area during your book signing party.

Types of sponsored prizes are gift certificates: hair salons, nail service, or hair services; ju-jitsu classes, 30-minute free massages from chiropractors, etc. You can get a bunch of different donations from local businesses that want to help and sponsor you.

This will make it fun and exciting. Of course, you'll want to plan to have a drink or food, and you'll attract even more people. One thing that I always do is to either cater or ask for donation from a local bakery or any type of yummy treat that will attract people to come.

When selecting a location for a book signing party or a book launch party, consider locations that might help bring you additional traffic. For instance, when seeking out a place to do this, understand that most businesses will have newsletter lists, social media following, etc. Ask them to promote your book signing party on their list.

They typically will be willing to do this because anyone that comes to your book signing party is coming to their place of business and therefore, may engage in additional buying activity with them. It also tends to make their business a more popular and busy location. Everybody likes to go where the "buzz" is, and a book signing party can help create some buzz for that business at that time.

When discussing a book launch party with a potential location, also let them know that you will be inviting local media to the book signing party as well. This will certainly give this potential business and/or location the understanding that they may have additional free press and advertising simply because of your event.

Also consider selecting a location that serves food themselves. For instance, if you hold the party at a restaurant, café, or something along these lines, you may not need to provide food because people will be able to buy it there. You may arrange some sort of discount with the business, so that people can come to the signing party and get some sort of promotional deal while at the business. This can apply not just to restaurants but really any kind of business.

Again, remember that "people support what they create." When discussing this potential signing party with the business, work with them to create something special and be open to ideas that they may have. Remember that some of these businesses have significant experience in promoting events at their business. Leverage this experience and take advantage of it.

When you are going to hold your event, they will be sending out a newsletter to their list, and you'll want to make sure that you have all the information and make it a fun and catchy invitation. A local quilt shop sent a newsletter to Jenn. She is on their email list, and they sent this:

Do something for your book anniversary, have a book signing every year!

This is critical for readers who have already launched books. Don't think that a book signing party is limited to your launch cycle. You can use a book signing party at anytime and anywhere to generate more interest in your book. While we are not tax professionals, we suspect that there might be some value in setting a book signing party in some place that you wish to go on a vacation to. Perhaps there would be some tax benefit to this, but we do recommend that you discuss this with your tax professional.

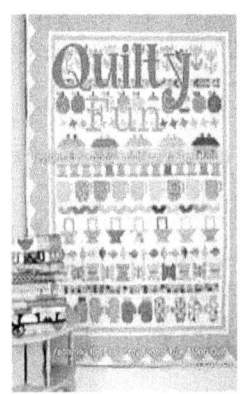

Book Signing
November 8th
11:00am - 1:00pm

Quilty Fun's 1st Anniversary

Lori Holt Book Signing at Thimbles and Threads

Lori Holt will be at Thimbles and Threads for a book signing this Sat. Nov. 8th, from 11 am - 1 pm to celebrate her book's 1st anniversary. She will be bringing her Quilty Fun projects for all to see.

Come join us for two hours of *Quilty Fun!* Lori will be signing books, patterns, and projects. Don't worry if you don't have a copy of her book, we will have copies for sale at the store.

20 - JOINT VENTURES

In the online marketing world, it is very common for two businesses or two individuals to get together and work on a joint project for joint profit. In many cases, this means one person leverages their list to benefit the other person. Let me give you an example.

Paulo Coelho is a very accomplished author internationally, but he was struggling to get penetration into the U.S. market. Mr. Coelho and online marketer Brendon Burchard got together and decided to participate in a joint venture. Mr. Coelho provided huge numbers of his book called Manuscript Found in Accra to Brendon Burchard.

Brendon Burchard, in turn, emailed his entire list and offered people Coelho's book for free if they only paid shipping and handling. There was a huge response to Burchard's promotion, and Mr. Coelho's books ended up being provided to countless people who had never heard of him or read any of his books. As a result, Coelho found his notoriety and impact in the United States magnified exponentially through this joint venture.

This is one way to operate a joint venture (JV). In this circumstance, don't assume for a minute that Coelho lost money in the joint venture, even initially. Selling a book for the cost of shipping and handling, depending upon the volume discount that the author got on the printing of the book, can be done at cost. We have seen this strategy employed several times where the cost of shipping and handling was as much as $10, when we know full well that the cost of the book to the author was probably under $5.

We have seen this strategy employed multiple times even in a launch cycle in order to help an author become a New York Times Bestselling author. A strategy like this was employed by Burchard to launch his own book *The Charge*, and a similar strategy was recently employed with Jeff Walker's book, *Launch*. In fact, Burchard has used this strategy several times in the last four or five years for his own books as well as others.

Now, think about what is in it for you if you participate in a joint venture. If you are the author, you can find people who have a list that you think will be receptive to your message and your products. Naturally, you don't want to waste your time doing this with someone who has a list that is not part of your target market or avatar.

Instead, find somebody that is already marketing to your audience, somebody that is already selling products to your audience. Get in touch with them and figure out a way that you can do a joint venture together. There are many ways to structure such a joint venture. You could give your books away for free and have that person mail their list or promote your book.

Then you could share in follow-up sales or backend sales, giving a percentage of sales to that person who promoted to their list. You could also sell your book at retail or whatever price directly to that person's list and divide profits according to your agreement. You might also find ways to joint venture on a quid pro quo basis where that person markets your product to his or her list, and you market their products to your list.

There really are unlimited ways to structure this. You could always allow that person to come and speak at your event, if you can sell your books and products to their list. They may have you come and speak at their event and take a portion of your sales from whatever you sell from the stage. The JV world really is endless.

A word of caution is in order. As with any partnership, make sure that you and your JV partner understand in advance everything that's going to happen with this joint venture and particularly how profits are going to be divided. And for that matter, will the resources be divided net or will they be provided off of the gross? What timeframe is going to be employed with the dispersal of profits? Who is going to handle the shopping cart or credit card fees? If some disagreement should come up, how will that disagreement be resolved?

We recommend that you consider employing a detailed contract and perhaps the services of an attorney if you are going to get involved in joint ventures in a serious way. At the same time, we are completely comfortable getting involved in joint ventures on a handshake or on a verbal agreement. In fact, this book came about simply because of a conversation. We don't believe a contract is always necessary, but we do caution you to consider one when significant amounts of money are on the line.

BONUS CHAPTERS

Yes, we know our book is subtitled the top TWENTY ways to make money with your book, but we just couldn't help ourselves! You see, once we sat down to write the book, we just couldn't stop!

So here are a few more ways to make money with your book. Some of these are ways to *leverage* your book to make money in other ways, and such ways are often the most profitable ways to make money through publishing.

We hope you find these bonus chapters to be helpful!

21 - INCREASE YOUR FEES

When talking about ways to make money from your book, it's important to remember that some of the best ways to make money from your book aren't involving book sales at all. Becoming an author puts you in an exclusive class and makes you something that you weren't prior to the launch of your book.

As a result, you will now be seen through different lenses, as it were, by your prospects and customers. Very few people can say that they have an author, let alone an Amazon bestselling author, working for them. Consider how unusual it would be to say that your financial planner, plumber, accountant, dentist, or exercise therapist is a bestselling author. Your authorship and your bestseller status should allow you to increase your fees, often substantially.

We both have clients that we have seen raise their fees substantially post authorship. We have seen clients raise their speaking fees by as much as 50% following the launch of their book. We personally have raised our fees post book launches. We also know other authors in various online communities that have seen their fees double and sometimes triple because of their books, and the additional leverage and authority that has come from launching their books.

If you are considering raising your fees with existing clientele, make sure to tread lightly, but at the same time, don't be timid. You deserve to get paid more because of your authority and exposure. One way to do this is to have a conversation with your clients along the lines of the following script:

Perhaps when renewing a contract with an existing client, you say something along these lines, "You know, Susie, I've had great success with the launch of the book, and we are getting a lot of attention because we were able to get that Amazon bestseller status. As a result, I really have a lot of potential clients coming out of the woodwork, and my fees have increased with them as a result. At the same time, I want to reward you for your loyalty and your business in the past. Therefore, though our fees have gone up by 30% for new clients, I am willing to renew your existing contract with a 10% or 15% increase instead. I hope you understand; with more business out there coming to us, we need to price ourselves accordingly."

Along the lines of keeping your current clients, after Jenn had her book with Dan Kennedy or the book *Stand Apart*, she did decide to raise her fees; however, for her current clients, she let them know that she would keep the current pricing and fee schedule as per the agreement, and for those that the agreement had run out, for the new agreement, she kept the same fees. Although with all the new clients, the fees were raised to 30% or more. She let the customer know that they had been such a good client that she would keep the same fees.

This did a lot for her as far as credibility and for referrals. Her clients really respected her for doing that and in return have given her multiple referrals that signed on at the new pricing.

A friend of ours, Yael Cohen, experienced this same phenomenon. She recently wrote and launched a book about the rights of special needs children in school districts. She also educates parents in regards to their rights for special assistance at school. Her hourly fee has been the same for many years. After she launched her book, she attended a mastermind retreat. While there, other experts recommended that she increase her fees. She was scared to do this but decided that she would follow through with this recommendation from her mastermind friends. Nervously, she gave her new rates to all new clients that approached her, this of course after giving each of the clients a copy of her book. A funny thing happened. Not a single new client offered any objection. Not a single client has questioned her about the new pay rate, even though it represents a 50% increase in her old hourly rate. You can do the same thing!

Therefore, you can see that you really can go either way with your prices. You can leave them intact for your existing customers if you wish to leverage goodwill and potential referrals, or you can raise the fees. It has been our experience that people understand that with a book launch and with its success comes increased value to your services and, with that, increased fees.

Naturally, you will encounter some clients who will resist this price increase. That's fine. With your increased authority and exposure from your book, you may now have the freedom to leave behind some of your lower paying clients to accept the benefits of higher paying clients.

22 - CLOSE MORE DEALS

A book is a fantastic conversion strategy. What we mean by this is a book will help you to convert potential leads into customers or clients and help you close more deals. There are many different tools available to us in

whatever industry we are in. Some tools are designed to bring us more leads; other tools are designed to help us close these leads; still others are designed to help us close those leads at a higher value. A book very easily accomplishes all three.

As an author, you have additional credibility and authority. With this additional credibility and authority comes a position that your competition lacks. In most circumstances, your competition does not have a book and is not a bestselling author. The fact that you have a book and perhaps are a bestselling author often eliminates competition entirely.

Consider this scenario for a moment. Let's say you are seeking a social media consultant to do Facebook marketing for your business. You interview three or four different consultants as you consider how you wish to proceed. One of those consultants happens to be an Amazon bestselling author of a book on Facebook marketing.

While we recognize that you are going to consider numerous factors, on the face of this, which consultant are you most likely to pursue to work with you? And which consultant are you more likely to be willing to pay more money to? Naturally, it's the one with the book. Now we know that the book by itself won't close the deal, but a book will automatically put your prospects and your buyers in a position where they are predisposed to do business with you.

Everyone wants to have an expert working for them. Everybody wants their expert to be the best one possible or at least the best one that they can afford. If you have a book, and particularly a bestselling book, then you are likely to be that expert that they seek out.

Following the launch of Everett's book, *The Video Tractor Beam*, Everett was approached by several people to get videos produced. Everett's book isn't at all about video production; it is really only about video marketing. However, because Everett was now the Amazon Bestselling author of a book on video marketing, he was immediately seen by these prospects as expert in the area of video production as well.

Incidentally, Everett and his team went ahead and produced these videos with great success. But the important lesson here is that the book positioned Everett and his team as experts, and immediately made prospects inclined to do business with them. It should also be noted that those prospects never approached any other video production company to discuss their videos. They simply saw Everett as an expert, and they assumed that Everett could take care of their needs.

In Jenn's launch of her book *Video Marketing for Professionals*, she received multiple emails and conversations on Facebook after launching the book, and many people wanted to meet with her to talk about their books. Because of her success and her #1 bestseller, she booked meetings and closed deals with these authors and potential authors.

23 - PRE-LAUNCHING BOOKS

During the writing of this book, Amazon has given self-publishing authors the ability to pre-launch their books. In essence, this gives an author a chance to put a book for sale on Amazon before the book is even written. This really is a wonderful opportunity to generate revenue for your book, even before you have taken significant steps to write your book.

You can put your book out for sale several months in advance and then go through the steps of creating your book.

You can set whatever price you deem appropriate. You can also alter that price later. One caution here though, if you should lower your book price during your pre-launch period, Amazon may apply that reduced price later to all your buyers. Therefore, do this very carefully unless you are comfortable with your previous buyers getting your book at a reduced cost as well. At present, this pre-launch option is available only on the Kindle Direct Publishing platform.

It is difficult for us to know the longevity of this pre-order option because Amazon has had some problems with people moving their launch dates. We have also seen where authors have received an "Amazon slap" for moving such dates.

A friend of ours asked to move his launch date back by one day because of some challenges with editing and graphics. Amazon was gracious enough to allow him to move his launch back by one day, but they also removed the pre-launch option from his account for one year. Other punishments could be in the offing as well if pre-launch is abused.

We know multiple authors that have employed pre-launch to get that selling status before their book was ever completed. Keep in mind that Amazon will count book sales on the day that the person pre-orders the book. They will not gather up the sales and process them on launch date; instead they will typically process them at the exact time that the person clicks the button to pre-order the book. This is good and bad.

It's bad if you're hoping to gather up all your pre-launch sales and have them count on one day for ranking. It's good if you recognize that you can do a launch cycle during a pre-launch period in the same way that you would have during a normal launch, focusing people's pre-purchase activities onto one day for ranking purposes.

Ultimately, using the pre-launch can be a great way to generate revenue from a book and even pay you to write that book if you can get enough people to buy it during the pre-launch period.

CONCLUSION

We hope this book will help you make money with your book. We have used many, if not all, of these ideas to help propel our businesses forward. Having a book and becoming a bestselling author is a big accomplishment. We are so proud of everyone reading this book that has taken this action. We would love to answer any of your questions about publishing or writing a book. If you haven't done so, please register your book and you will receive more information and bonuses to help you in the future.

Register This Book and Get Free Updates and a Money Mind Map

Things change rapidly in the publishing world! If you register your copy of this book, we will keep you up to date about the ever-changing ways to leverage your book. PLUS, we will send you our custom infographic, your "mind map" for making money with a book!

Visit AuthorJennFoster.com/books-to-bucks

ABOUT THE AUTHORS

Everett O'Keefe is a Wall Street Journal, USA Today, and International #1 Bestselling Author. The Power of the Published is his most recent solo work. He has also helped create and launch more than 100 bestselling books for his clients. Everett speaks across the nation on the power of publishing. He is the founder of Ignite Press, a hybrid publishing company that specializes in helping entrepreneurs, as well as business and medical professionals, ignite their businesses by becoming bestselling authors.

Everett is the winner of multiple awards, including the Publish and Profit Award for Excellence in Publishing, the Make Market & Launch It Award for Product Creation, and the Top Gun Consulting Award, among others. He is the co-founder of the Business Accelerator Group, a high-level mastermind group composed of international marketers and publishers. He also founded the Mastermind Retreat and hosts international mastermind events.

In 2019, Everett founded The Book Publishers Network, a group of publishers, publishing consultants, book coaches and other book professionals. In 2020, he founded The Publishers Mastermind to help support publishing professionals from around the world.

Everett is sought out as a speaker, coach, and consultant by authors and marketing experts worldwide. With a passion for entrepreneurialism, Everett helps his clients become recognized experts in their fields through speaking and authorship while allowing his clients to focus on their own areas of giftedness.

You can reach Everett through his company's website at
IgnitePress.us
Facebook.com/ignitepress
Linkedin.com/in/everettokeefe
Amazon.com/author/everettokeefe

Other Books by Everett O'Keefe:
Authority: Strategic Concepts from 15 International Thought Leaders to Create Influence, Credibility and a Competitive Edge for You and Your Business

My New Book: The Upcoming Message That Will Change the World!

The Power of the Published: How Rapidly Authoring a Book Can Ignite Your Business and Your Life

The Video Tractor Beam: Dominate Your Field and At- tract New Clients and Customers with Online Video

There's Money in This Book: 17 Secrets from a Marketing Mastermind

Your Epic Book Launch: How to Write a Book, Launch It to a #1 International Bestseller, Raise Your Income, Make Money Online, and Build a 6 to 7 Figure Business, Even If You Don't Know How

Jenn Foster is a Wall Street Journal, USA Today, and International Bestselling Author. She is the owner of Elite Online Publishing and Biz Social Marketing Agency. Companies dedicated to helping business owners of all sizes thrive in today's highly technical world of product and service promotion. Jenn owned and operated a successful local chain of retail stores, where she honed her online marketing skills. From local brick and mortar stores to online entities, to large international corporations, Jenn's years of experience and expertise has now helped hundreds of businesses become front-page news on major search engines. She is dedicated to helping businesses use powerful new online and mobile marketing platforms to get visibility, traffic, leads, customers, and raving fans. She is passionate about helping busy entrepreneurs, business leaders, and professionals to create, publish, and market their book, to build their business and brand. She encourages new authors to share their stories, knowledge and expertise to help others. With her marketing and digital background, Jenn uses the best strategies for her client's books to boost their sales and marketing platforms and helps them achieve #1 bestselling status.

A graduate of Utah State University, Jenn is an award-winning web designer, author, and sought-after speaker. She has been a featured panelist and speaker at events with experts like Loral Langemeier, Lisa Sasevich, Mike Koenigs, Ed Rush, and more. Jenn has been named one of America's Premier Experts® and is highlighted in the Dan Kennedy Book, Stand Apart. Jenn Foster was recently named one of "Utah's Thought Leaders" in the book Innovate Utah by Global Village. Jenn is the co-host of Elite Expert Insider Podcast on iTunes and Spotify.

Coming from a family of successful entrepreneurs, her grandfather started the Maverik Country Stores oil and gas station chain which is still thriving today. Jenn grew up around successful businesses and understands from the ground up what it takes to create, run, and promote winning companies. Combining her education, knowledge, and life-long experience, today Jenn teaches people and businesses globally connect and follow up with prospects to convert them to customers. how they can get found in today's virtual world, how they can engage prospects on their terms and how to continue to

Jenn is a single Mom who loves spending time with her three children, traveling, and experiencing the great outdoors.

Follow Jenn Foster:

BizSocialMarketing.com

AuthorJennFoster.com

Eliteonlinepublishing.com

Facebook.com/authorjennfoster

@jennfosterchic

Instagram.com/eliteonlinepublishing

YouTube.com/elilteonlinepublishing1

LinkedIn.com/in/jennfosterseo

Podcasts:
Elite Expert Insider

Elite Publishing Podcast

Courses:
BookWritingFastPass.com

BestsellerSolutions.com

BookLaunchTraining.com

Other Books by Jenn Foster:
Authority: Strategic Concepts from 15 International Thought Leaders to Create Influence, Credibility and a Competitive Edge for You and Your Business

Podcast Authorized: Turn Your Podcast Into a Book That Builds Your Business

7 Costly Mistakes When Choosing a Publisher: Self Publishing Secrets That Will Save You Thousands

How to Write Your Life Story and Leave a Legacy: A Story Starter Guide to Write your Autobiography and Memoir (2nd Edition)

How To Write Your Story of Success to Impact the World: A Story Starter Guide to Write Your Business or Personal Stories, Goals, and Achievements (2nd Edition)

How to Write and Capture Your Family Yearbook and Story: A Story Starter Guide to Write Your Family Stories of the Year (2nd Edition)

Stand Apart: with Dan Kennedy

Famous Inspirational Quotes: Over 100 Motivational Quotes for Life Positivity

Schreiber Cookbook: Everyday and Gourmet Recipes Spanning Four Generations

www.ingramcontent.com/pod-product-compliance
Lightning Source LLC
LaVergne TN
LVHW011950070526
838202LV00054B/4884